Garfield chews the fat

BY: JIM DAVIS

BALLANTINE BOOKS • NEW YORK

Library of Congress Catalog Card Number: 88-92024

ISBN: 0-345-35956-9

Manufactured in the United States of America

First Edition: March 1989

10 9 8 7 6 5 4 3 2 1

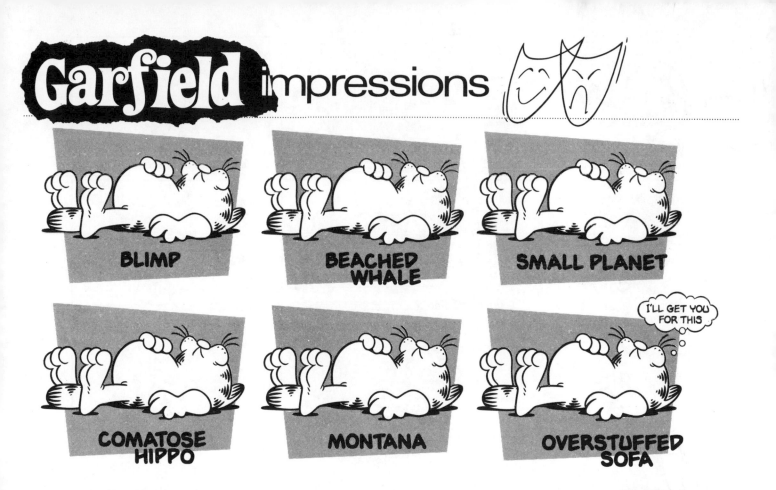

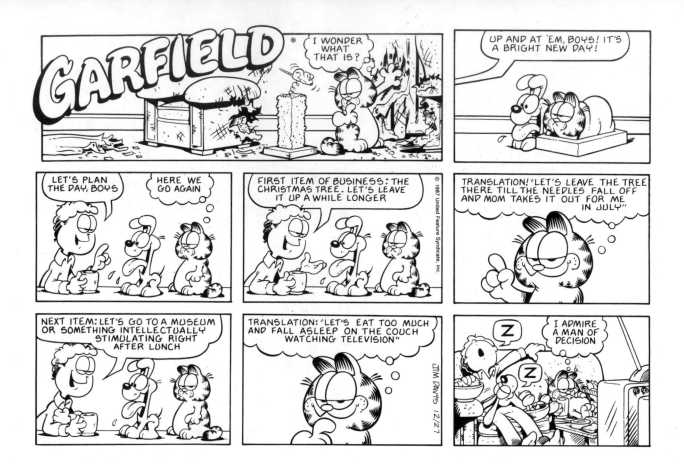

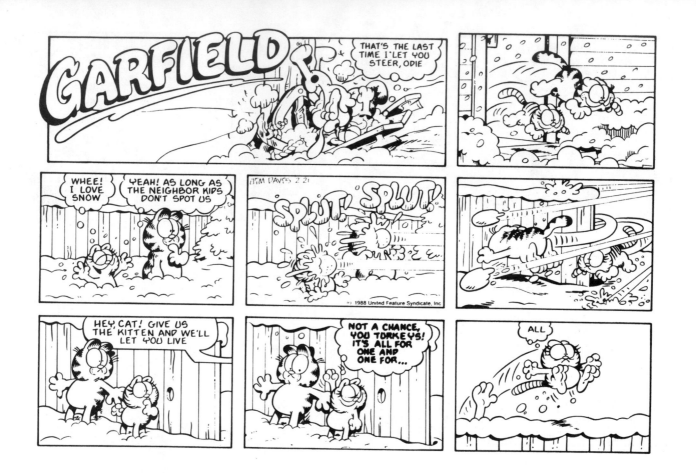

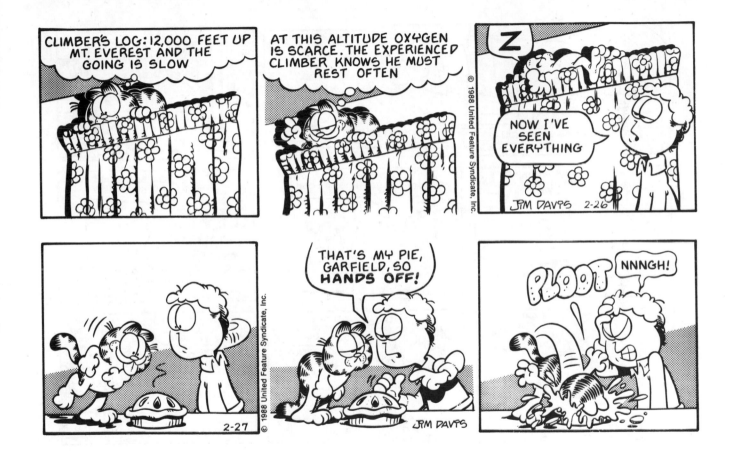

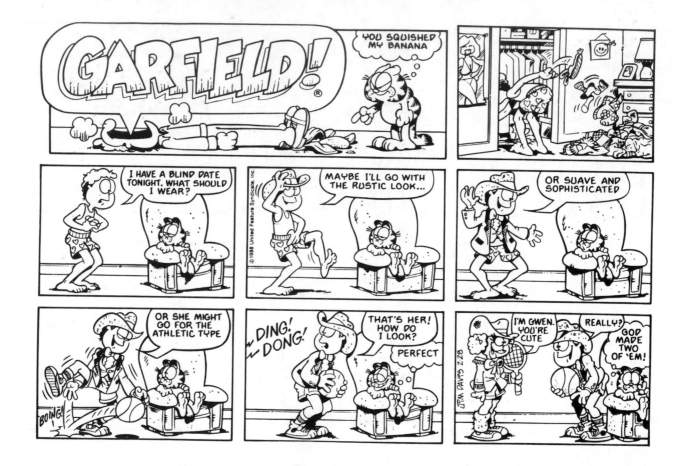

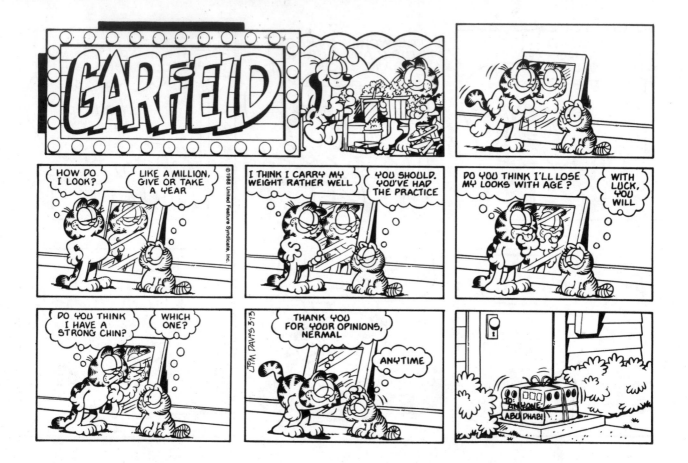

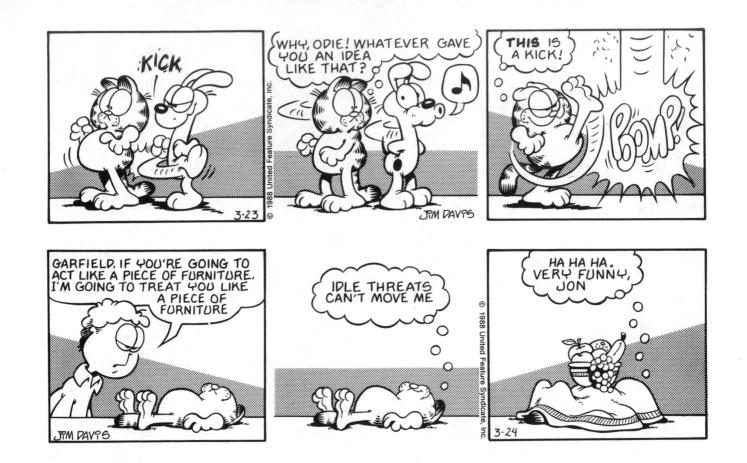

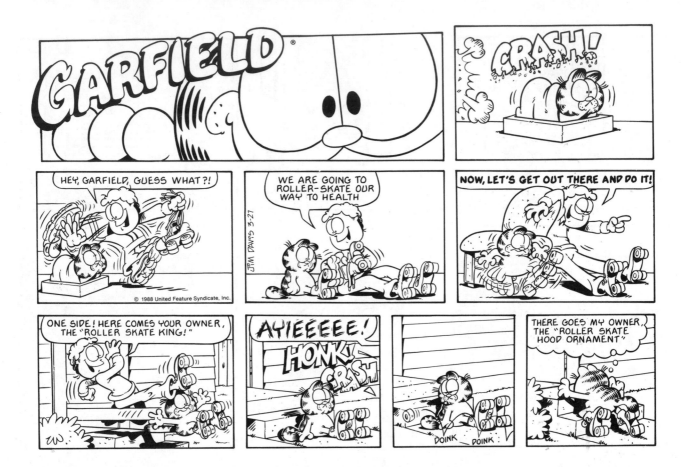

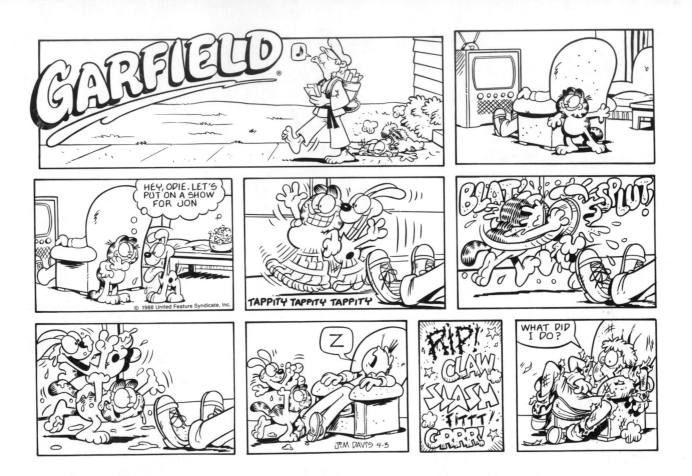

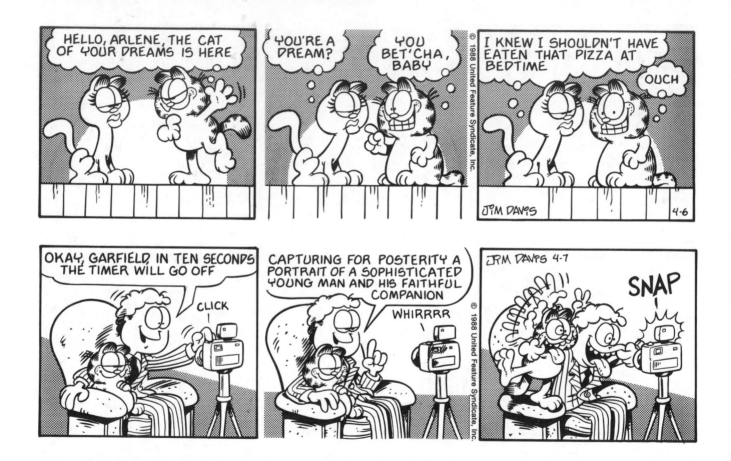

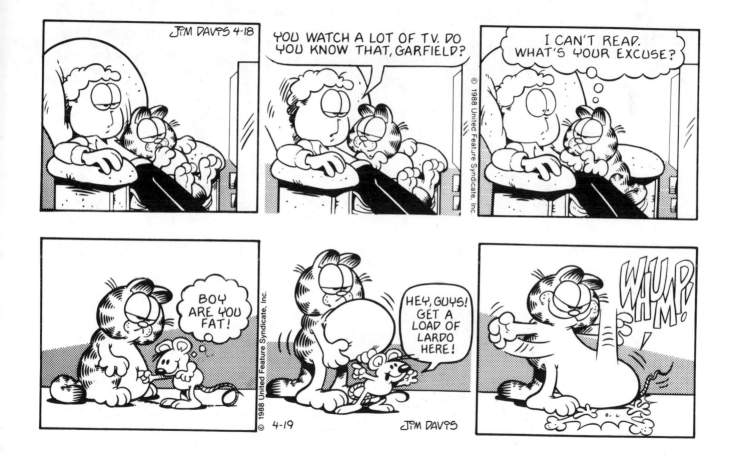

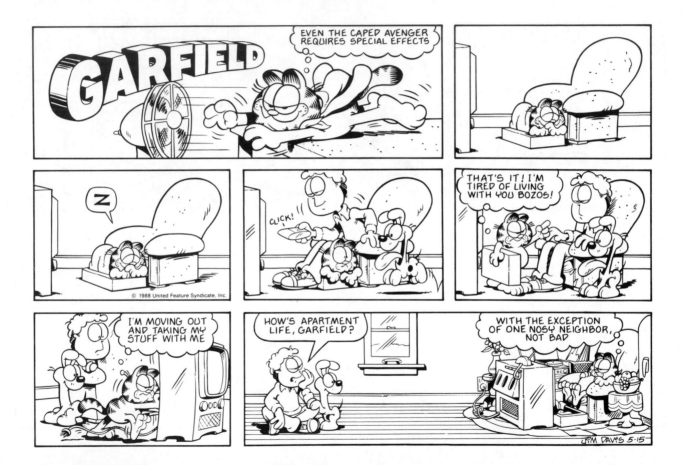

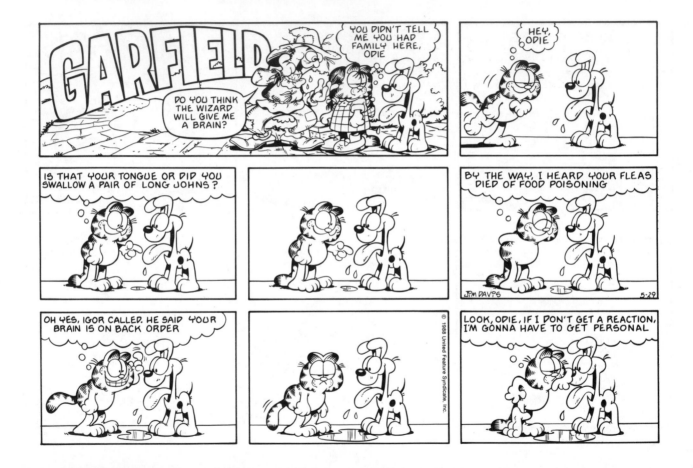

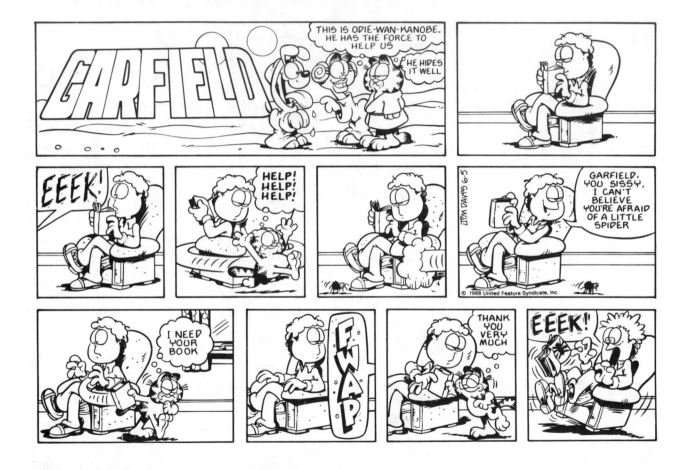

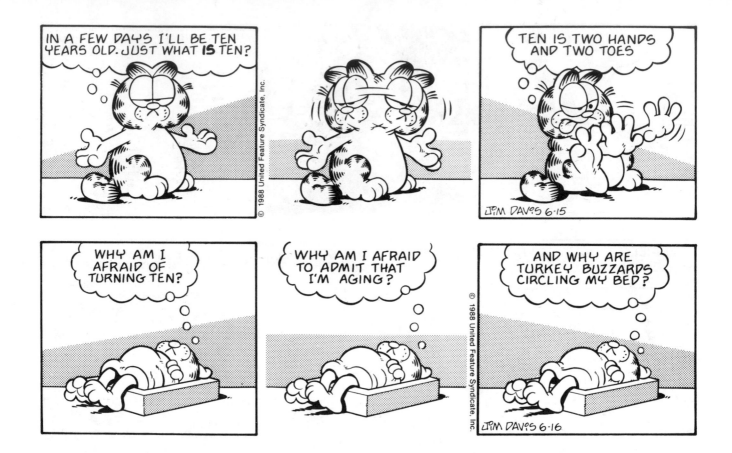

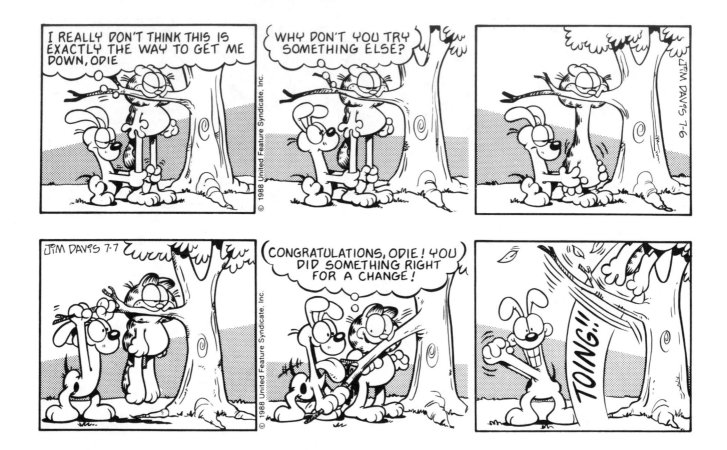

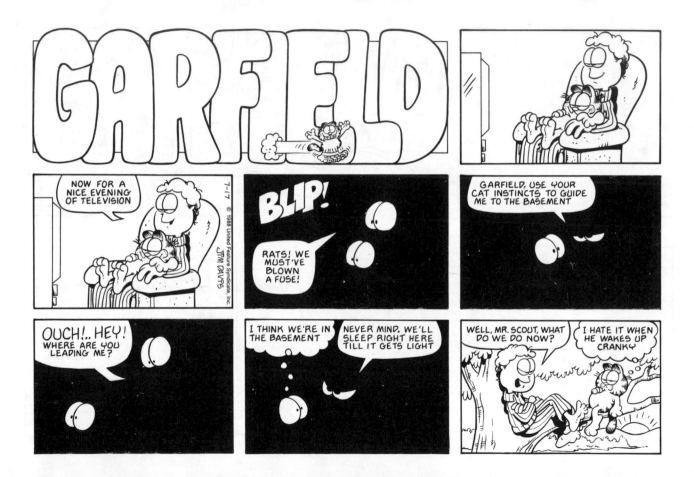

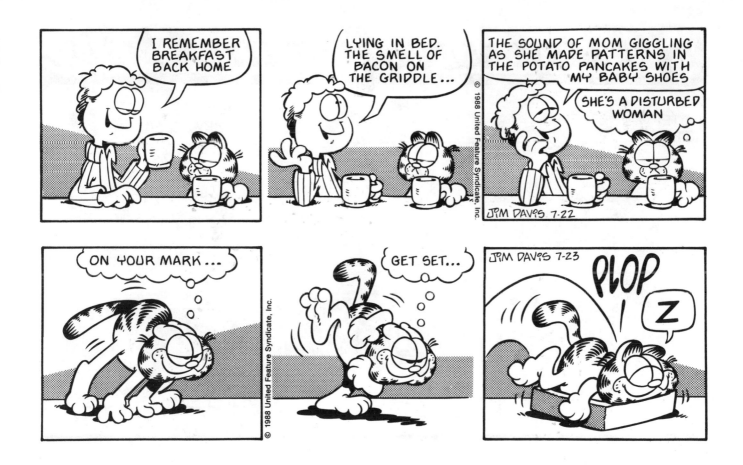